I dedicate this book
to my children and grandchildren,
who are the love of my life
and have shared in my rebirth
renewing my hope for a
better future for all.

I thank my family
for their encouragement
and help in bringing this
remembrance book to life.

A Note About The Artist

Holocaust survivor Ms. Hanka Kornfeld-Marder was born in Bendzin, Poland, in 1928. In 1941, at the young age of 13, she was taken on a transport train to Auschwitz. The train transporting her, remained at the railroad tracks at the station for three days and three nights, before being moved along to other camps. She was saved because Auschwitz, at the time, was too crowded to accept any more prisoners. Over the next four years, Hanka Kornfeld-Marder was an inmate in four German concentration camps – Faulbrück, Reichenbach, Langbilau, and Peterswaldau – before being liberated on May 8, 1945.

After the war, Ms. Kornfeld-Marder settled in Santiago, Chile, where she raised a family, developed and managed a jewelry business and studied painting. Her paintings have their own set of feelings and emotions, that both capture and touch the heart, establishing that special link between past, present and her hopes for a better future for humanity.

Her first "Holocaust Collection", with 20 paintings was completed between 1979 and 1982 and was displayed in Valparaiso, Concepcion and Santiago, Chile. The second series of 23 oil on canvas paintings, composed between 1982 and 1984, constitutes the Collection "My Paintings, My Memories, My Message…" This collection made its world premiere at the Starr Gallery, in Newton, Massachusetts, USA on April 8,1985, on the occasion of the 40th anniversary of the liberation of the concentration camps at the end of World War II.

Ms. Hanka Kornfeld-Marder was one of four Holocaust Survivors whose art was displayed as part of the "The Art of Survivors" exhibit held at the Lobby of the United Nations Headquarters in New York City in 2007. Her painting, "The Death Train Arrives in Auschwitz", painted in 1982, was portrayed as the face of the exhibit.

Children Before Entering The Concentration Camp

Holocaust Collection

23 x 28 | Oil On Canvas | 1981

Grandmother And Granddaughter: Their Painful Farewell Before Entering The Auschwitz Crematoria

Collection | My Paintings, My Memories, My Message...

17 x 21 | Oil On Canvas | 1982

Kristalnacht

Collection | My Paintings, My Memories, My Message…

19 x 25 | Oil On Canvas | 1984

Grandmother Enters The Auschwitz Gas Chamber

Collection | My Paintings, My Memories, My Message...

21 x 25 | Oil On Canvas | 1982

The Window: Fear Starvation And Darkness

Holocaust Collection

20 x 22 | Oil On Canvas | 1980

The Death Train Arrives In Auschwitz

Collection | My Paintings, My Memories, My Message…

33 x 24 | Oil On Canvas | 1983

Mother In Despair Behind The Bars Of The Concentration Camp

Holocaust Collection

31 x 24 | Oil On Canvas | 1982

Escape: The Last Chance

Collection | My Paintings, My Memories, My Message…

19 x 25 | Oil On Canvas | 1984

An Anguished Mother And Son Await Their Turn To Die In The Gas Chambers

Collection | My Paintings, My Memories, My Message…

19 x 25 | Oil On Canvas | 1983

The Death Train Arrives In Auschwitz

Collection | My Paintings, My Memories, My Message…

25 x 19 | Oil On Canvas | 1982

Hanging On: The Will To Survive

Collection | My Paintings, My Memories, My Message…

17 x 21 | Oil On Canvas | 1984

Anguish At The Ruins of The Concentration Camp

Collection | My Paintings, My Memories, My Message…

19 x 25 | Oil On Canvas | 1983

Praying, Asking For The Miracle To Stay Alive In The Camp

Holocaust Collection

23 x 28 | Oil On Canvas | 1981

The Train: Voyage Without Hope To The Auschwitz Crematoria

Collection | My Paintings, My Memories, My Message…

25 x 16 | Oil On Canvas | 1983

Looking From The Window Of The Concentration Camp

Holocaust Collection

28 x 23 | Oil On Canvas | 1981

Auschwitz. The Flames Consume The Human Beings

Holocaust Collection

28 x 23 | Oil On Canvas | 1981

Fear

Collection | My Paintings, My Memories, My Message…

25 x 37 | Oil On Canvas | 1983

Farewell Between Father And Son Before Entering The Auschwitz Gas Chambers

Collection | My Paintings, My Memories, My Message…

27 x 23 | Oil On Canvas | 1982

Slow Agony In The Bunks Beds Of The Concentration Camp

Holocaust Collection

17 x 21 | Oil On Canvas | 1981

At The Border Of Death

Holocaust Collection

20 x 23 | Oil On Canvas | 1980

A Mother, Her Sister, And Her Two Sons Arrive On The Train At The Auschwitz Crematoria

Collection | My Paintings, My Memories, My Message…

26 x 18 | Oil On Canvas | 1983

Mother and Son In The Ruins Of Auschwitz

Collection | My Paintings, My Memories, My Message…

25 x 19 | Oil On Canvas | 1982

Mother And Her Son Await Their Deaths in The Crematoria

Collection | My Paintings, My Memories, My Message…

21 x 27 | Oil On Canvas | 1982

The Train To Auschwitz

Collection | My Paintings, My Memories, My Message…

14 x 17 | Oil On Canvas | 1983

After so many years my hopes and dreams for peace still resonate deep inside my soul. I yearn for a peaceful world, without discrimination, a world that shall never forget the millions of innocent people who suffered during the Holocaust. My hope is for the future, for my grandchildren to live in a world that I did not see.

With this Holocaust Remembrance Book of Paintings I plead to the next generation, to remember the images they see and to became messengers of understanding, tolerance and peace. If one ignores the Holocaust, they condone these actions to repeat themselves.

It is with all my heart I wish to leave you, the reader, with hope for the future. The future of the world lies directly in your hands now. The world can be molded with love and understanding, in any direction that you wish.

We must never forget those who were murdered, we must never forget those who survived and we must never forget the heroes of the Holocaust. We honor them by remembering and by never allowing a dark cloud of evil to ever cover our hope for peace under the sun. I wish for the world to never forget and for the sun to always shine through the clouds and illuminate our world at peace.

H.K.M.